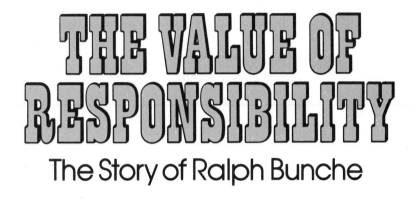

THE VALUE OF RESPONSIBILITY

The Story of Ralph Bunche

VALUE COMMUNICATIONS, INC.
PUBLISHERS
LA JOLLA, CALIFORNIA

THE VALUE OF RESPONSIBILITY

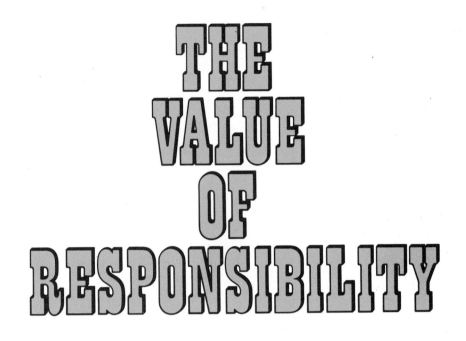

The Story of
Ralph Bunche

BY ANN DONEGAN JOHNSON

First Edition
Manufactured in the United States of America
For information write to: ValueTales, P.O. Box 1012
La Jolla, CA 92038

Library of Congress Cataloging in Publication Data

Johnson, Ann Donegan.
    The value of responsibility.

    (ValueTales)
    1.   Bunche, Ralph Johnson, 1904-1971—Juvenile literature.   2.   Statesmen—United States—Biography—Juvenile literature.   3.   Responsibility—Juvenile literature.   I.   Title.
E748.B885J63   341.23'3'0924 [B]   78-13960

ISBN 0-916392-29-5

This tale is about a very responsible person, Ralph Bunche. The story that follows is based on events in his life. More historical facts about Ralph Bunche can be found on page 63.

Once upon a time...

not so very long ago as we measure these things, a little boy named Ralph Bunche lived in a tumbledown house in the heart of Detroit's Negro district.

Ralph lived with his family, of course, and he had quite a big family. First of all there was skinny, brave little Grandma Johnson. Then there were Ralph's parents—his gentle, soft-spoken father, Fred, and his mother, Olive Agnes. Ralph's Aunt Nelle lived with them, and so did Aunt Ethel. And my! How everyone worked!

Ralph's father worked in the barbershop on the first floor of the tumbledown house. He gave haircuts for a dime and shaves for a nickel.

But it took lots of dimes and nickels—and quarters and half dollars and dollars—to keep such a big family going. So Ralph's mother worked, and the aunts worked, and Grandma Johnson worked, too. Sometimes the women went out to their jobs. Sometimes they brought their work home.

Once Ralph came in and found his mother and Grandma Johnson sitting at the table sewing. They were making doll dresses for the toy factory nearby. "We'll get twenty cents for every dress we finish," said Grandma Johnson. "That's good money—if we work fast enough."

Ralph worked, too, even though he was only seven. Every day after school he sold newspapers on a street corner. "Extra!" he shouted. "Read all about it! Get your daily paper!"

When he'd finished selling his papers, Ralph took his little pile of pennies and nickels home and heaped them up on the table so that Grandma could count them. Some weeks he made more than a dollar.

"Isn't that great?" cried Ralph. "I'm doing my share!"

Grandma just smiled, and she never tried to stop Ralph or tell him not to work so hard. In most families in those days, everybody had to do what they could to help the family get along.

Before long, Ralph discovered that he couldn't sell too many papers if he stayed in the Negro district. Not many black people had enough money to afford a newspaper.

"All right," said Ralph to himself. "I won't stay here. I'll go out to neighborhoods where the people have more money."

Ralph walked until he found a place called Cadillac Square. He saw theaters there, and fine shops, and crowds of people dressed in fancy clothes.

"This is where I should be," thought Ralph as he stood at the curb. "Paper!" he cried. "Get your daily paper!"

He was very young and very courageous, and lots of the elegant people bought papers from him.

13

Ralph was happy and excited when he went home that night. He had a great pile of pennies and nickels and dimes for Grandma Johnson. He had stories to tell, too, about the ladies he had seen in their stylish gowns and sleek furs, and the men in glossy hats and fine suits.

"That's how some folks live," said Grandma Johnson. "But what you wear isn't really important. What's really important is how you feel about yourself."

Then Grandma told Ralph about his grandfather, Ralph Johnson. "You're named for him," she said, "and he was born a slave. Being born a slave—that's nothing to be ashamed about. Never be ashamed of what you are, Ralph. Be proud, like your granddaddy was. He was a fine man, and if you do right, someday you're going to be something special, too."

Grandma gave Ralph a hug then, and sent him off to bed. And she went back to her sewing.

15

Ralph wasn't always working. He had school and homework, of course, and he sold his newspapers. Yet he always found time to play street games with the other boys. Broomstick baseball was their favorite. But the games didn't always go smoothly. Sometimes there were fights.

"I was safe by a mile!" shouted one boy one afternoon.

"Go on!" yelled another. "You were out!"

"Wow!" said Ralph. "What we need is an umpire!"

"Oh, I don't know about that!" said a small voice close to Ralph.

Ralph turned. Standing near him and leaning on a fence was a little fellow in a blue suit and cap.

"Just call me Ump," said the little man. He pushed his face mask up on top of his head so that Ralph could see his dark, mischievous eyes. He had a wide smile, just like Ralph's. In fact, he looked very much like Ralph.

"You're a smart boy," said the little man. "You know which side is right and which side is wrong, so why do you need an umpire to settle your arguments? Settle them yourself!"

Ralph grinned. He knew there really wasn't a little man in a blue suit leaning on the fence. He knew that he had imagined Ump, and when he listened to Ump talk, he was simply listening to his own thoughts. Just the same, Ralph liked the idea of a let's-pretend friend. When the ball game was over, Ralph took Ump home with him.

19

"What a busy place!" said Ump, when he saw the tumbledown house where Ralph lived. Ralph's mother and his aunts were stitching away at dolls' dresses, and Grandma Johnson was cooking dinner.

"What do *you* do to help?" asked Ump.

"I sell papers," said Ralph. "When I'm bigger, I'll do more."

"I bet you will," said Ump. "You're a responsible boy."

"Responsible?" Ralph echoed. He had heard the word, but he hadn't really thought about it until now. "What does 'responsible' mean?" he asked. And he asked it out loud.

Grandma Johnson was at the stove and she heard him. "When you see what needs to be done and you do it, that's responsible," she told Ralph. "Why'd you ask that?"

"Oh, I met a new friend today," said Ralph. "He told me I was responsible."

21

In the days that followed, Ump went everywhere with Ralph. Ump and Ralph talked about everything. One day they talked about the people Ralph saw when he sold papers in Cadillac Square. "It isn't fair," said Ralph to Ump. "The ladies there have beautiful clothes and they ride in expensive carriages. But my grandma and mother and aunts have to work so hard!"

"Don't let it get you," warned Ump. "It will only hurt *you* if you get angry. Just keep being responsible. Keep doing what needs to be done, and things will get better."

22

So Ralph didn't let himself become angry or sad, and he kept on doing what had to be done. He kept working and studying. Between times he played baseball. And he always helped Grandma.

Then, when Ralph was ten, there were changes in the family.

Ralph's baby sister Grace was born. Ralph took turns with Grandma and the aunts helping look after her. His mother couldn't always see to the baby, for she was ill. Ralph's father was sick, too. He coughed all the time. Soon he couldn't work.

"Mrs. Bunche has rheumatic fever," the doctor told Grandma. "And Mr. Bunche—well, he has tuberculosis."

In those days many black people had tuberculosis. There were no miracle drugs to cure the disease, and there weren't many free clinics to help poor people when they got sick.

"We've got to do something," said Ralph, "and whatever we do, it will probably cost money."

Ump sighed. "Everything does," he agreed.

One night not long after this, Ralph came home and found Grandma and the aunts sitting at the table. Over and over again, Grandma was counting a little stack of money. She looked very serious.

"We're going to leave here," she told Ralph. "We're going to Albuquerque, New Mexico. It's warm and sunny there, and the air is dry. Maybe there your momma can get better. And maybe your daddy won't cough so much. We'll go as soon as we have enough money for the train fare."

"I knew it!" said Ralph to Ump. "I knew we'd need extra money. And I'm not making enough selling papers. I've got to do more. Maybe if I skip school . . ."

"Hold it!" shouted Ump. "Just a second here! Sure you've got a responsibility to your family. But you have to be responsible to yourself, too. If you start skipping school, what will you be for the rest of your life? A dunce?"

Ralph knew Ump was right. Besides, Grandma would never let him give up school. So he did the next best thing. He gave up selling papers and began shining shoes.

Of course Grandma always managed to work, and so did Aunt Nelle and Aunt Ethel. Soon the family had enough money to pay for tickets to Albuquerque.

Ralph was terribly excited when they went to the station to board the train. He ran ahead of the others. "Come on!" he cried. "Hurry up!"

"Careful!" warned Ump. "That man in the uniform is watching you, and he looks grumpy as all get-out."

Indeed the conductor was scowling at Ralph. In those days, there were coaches on some trains that were called Jim Crow coaches. Black people had to ride in these coaches when they traveled. In some parts of the country there were Jim Crow sections on the public streetcars, too, and usually they were located at the back of the cars.

"Hey, boy!" said the conductor, when he saw Ralph begin to get aboard one of the regular coaches. "You can't ride there. Go on to the back of the train."

"That's not right!" said Ralph, when he and Ump were seated in the Jim Crow coach with the rest of the family.

"Of course it's not right," said Grandma, "but that's the way things are right now. Maybe some day it will be different."

"It had better be different," said Ralph. "People expect blacks to be responsible and pay for things they use. When we do, we ought to get what we've paid for."

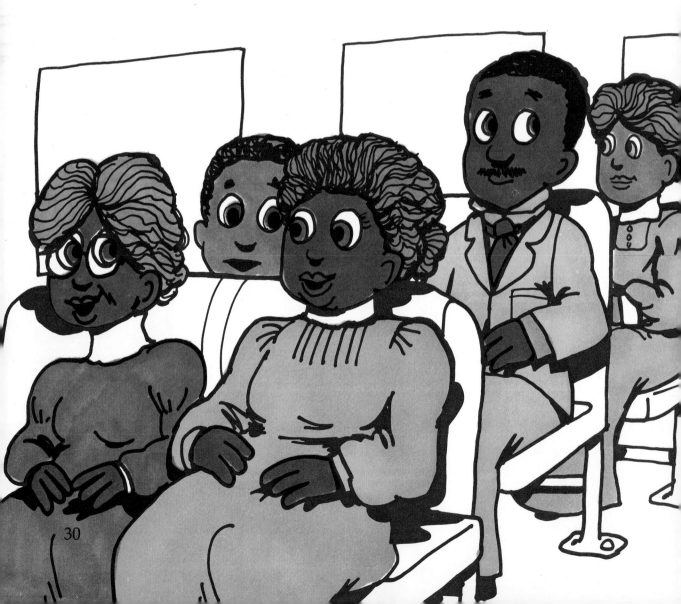

30

"Good for you!" cried Ump. "You're figuring it out! Responsibility works both ways. You've got to be responsible. You've got to do what needs doing. But you've got to see to it that other people treat you right!"

"If I can help it, I'll never ride in a Jim Crow coach again," Ralph said.

"I hope you never have to," said Ump.

The train rolled out of the station and sped across the countryside. Ralph watched. Then he slept. Then he woke again. And after it seemed to him that he had been riding for years—or for centuries—Ump nudged him.

"We're here!" cried Ump.

And they were in Albuquerque—which wasn't like any place Ralph had ever seen.

"That's an Indian!" cried Ralph, when he saw a tall brave in the railroad station. "A real, live Indian!"

"Did you think they only happened in history books?" asked Ump. Then he smiled when Ralph stared at the Mexican women who chattered with one another on the streets. Ralph waved to the brown-skinned boys who rode on burros.

"I think I'm going to like it here," said Ralph.

Ralph did like it. But when Grandma took him to the Fourth Ward Elementary School to enroll him, he was a bit nervous. There was only one other black student in his class.

"I think it may have been easier living back in Detroit," Ralph whispered to Ump. "There were more black kids."

But then the teacher came in. "My name is Miss Emma Sweet," she said, and she wrote her name on the board so that everyone could remember it. She had a nice smile, and when she talked to the students she looked them right in the eyes.

"I like her," said Ump in a low voice. "She looks like she's going to be fair. I'll bet it isn't going to make any difference to her at all that you're black."

Ump was right, as usual, for it didn't make any difference. Miss Sweet was a born teacher, and she knew how to bring out the best in her students. Ralph had always done well in school, but now he became really brilliant.

"You're just too perfect!" teased Ump.

But Ralph wasn't perfect. Not at all. When he finished his work ahead of the other students, he talked to the boy next to him. Sometimes he threw spitballs. And when he thought no one was looking, he slid down the bannister.

"You'll be sorry if Miss Sweet catches you," warned Ump.

And Ralph was sorry. Miss Sweet wanted her students to learn, but she also insisted that they behave. When Ralph acted up, she made him stand in a corner. And when the report cards came out, Ralph got a "C" in conduct.

Grandma wasn't too disappointed about that "C." Ralph was doing well in all of his subjects, and he was working, too, selling newspapers and helping people with their luggage down at the depot.

Grandma was working, too, of course. Grandma always worked. So did the aunts. Everyone worked. Everyone but the baby and Ralph's parents. Ralph's mother was very ill by now, and so was his father, and before they had been in Albuquerque much more than a year, Ralph's parents died.

The aunts cried, and Ralph cried too. But Grandma didn't cry much. She set to work, as Grandma always did, on the next thing that had to be done. This time her work was to make sure that Ralph finished his education.

"There's no use in staying in Albuquerque any more," she said. "We'll go to Los Angeles. There's more chance for a young person there."

And so the family was on the move again.

And when they got to Los Angeles, what do you suppose happened?

More school, of course. Ralph wasn't going to quit now.

More work, too. One summer Ralph got a job as a messenger in the offices of a newspaper, the *Los Angeles Times*. Another year he worked as a houseboy for a movie star. He grew bigger and stronger, and he moved vats in a factory where carpets were dyed.

Then, when he was 16, Ralph became a member of the debating team at Jefferson High School.

"You've got your nerve," said Ump. "Most black boys don't even stay in high school. And you? You're going out there to face an audience of white people!"

"I have to," said Ralph. "If I don't, how will they ever know we blacks are here?"

Ralph didn't stop with the debating team. He joined the baseball team, too, and the football team, and the basketball team. He made top marks in all of his subjects. He even won medals for debating and for English composition.

On graduation day, Ralph learned that he had won something more important than medals. "Grandma!" he cried. "They want to give me a scholarship to U.C.L.A.!"

But the instant Ralph said this, he was sorry. "I don't really want to go," he said quickly. "Most of the kids on our block didn't even finish high school. It's time I went to work full time and really earned some money."

"I've got a feeling," said Ump, "that Grandma isn't listening."

Grandma wasn't. When Ralph talked to her about his responsibilities, she just shook her head. "Your biggest responsibility is to yourself, Ralph Bunche," she said. "You're going to college so you can make something special of yourself—'cause you *are* something special!"

Now what do you suppose Ralph did?

Why he went to college, of course. He worked so hard and he studied so well that when he graduated he was given his degree "summa cum laude."

"Those sound like mighty important words," said Ump. "What do they mean?"

"They mean, 'with highest praise,'" said Ralph. "They mean I have the highest honors anyone can have when he graduates from college."

"And your grandma's so proud she could bust," said Ump. "Just wait till she hears you've got a fellowship and that you're going to go to Harvard University!"

"I knew you'd be something special," said Grandma, when Ralph told her the news.

Then one night, not long after, Grandma died quietly in her sleep. Ralph felt a terrible sadness.

"Don't worry," said Ump. "You made her very happy. Now go on and do your best. She would want that. All the dreams she had were for you."

45

So Ralph went to Harvard. And there, for the first time, he met other educated black people. Most of them were students, and they were just as poor as Ralph. But they all had great plans for the future. They met in the evenings, when classes were over and their work was done. They talked a lot about what it was like to be a Black in America.

Often the talks grew excited. Some evenings there were arguments that almost turned into fights.

"Hey!" cried Ump. "We really do need an umpire! Better do something, Ralph, before someone gets hurt!"

Ralph would jump into the argument then. And because he always knew what he was talking about, he didn't make any hasty, irresponsible remarks. So the others always calmed down and listened to him.

When Ralph finished his studies at Harvard, he accepted a teaching job at Howard University in Washington, D.C. This was the most famous Negro school in the country, and Ralph's classes were filled with bright, ambitious young black people.

Ralph was a good teacher, and he always had exciting things to talk about, so he was very popular. But he wasn't an easy teacher. He demanded that all his students do their best.

"That has something to do with responsibility, doesn't it?" asked Ump, when Ralph was marking papers one evening.

"It has everything to do with responsibility," declared Ralph. "If I do my best for the students but don't make sure they do their best too, then I haven't really accomplished anything. It isn't good for me and it isn't good for them."

Ralph got a faraway look in his eye just then.

"You're thinking of something nice, aren't you?" said Ump.

And he was.

49

He was thinking of Ruth Harris, a young lady who was one of his students. "Don't you think Ruth Harris is brighter than most of the class?" he asked Ump.

"I certainly do," said Ump. "Prettier, too. Or hadn't you noticed?"

But of course Ralph had noticed. The next day he asked Ruth to discuss a report with him. He talked and she listened. Then she talked and he listened. They met again and again, and before you know it, they were engaged.

Ralph had his job at Howard, but he didn't have much money. He had to work and scrimp and save until he had $150 to pay for their honeymoon. Then he and Ruth were married.

Just a year later, Ralph had a chance to go to Europe and Africa to study the problems of the people there. "It's a great opportunity," Ralph told Ruth, "but I don't think I can go. I don't want to leave you alone."

"Ralph, I knew when I married you that you would be an important man," said Ruth. "I know we'll have to be apart a lot. It's all right. You go on and do your studies."

"You sure married a nice lady," said Ump.

"I sure did," agreed Ralph, and he began his travels. In the years after his marriage, he went all over the world and studied the things that created differences and problems between people. He went back to Harvard to study, too, and he became the first black in America to get a doctor's degree in political science. His life was full and happy, and yet he was never too busy to dream.

"What we really need," he said to Ump, "is a place where people from every nation in the world can meet and talk—a place where they can discuss ways to settle their differences."

In 1941, the United States entered the Second World War, and Ralph became an adviser to the government. Then, in 1943, he became the first black to be named a division head in the Department of State.

"You're showing them something," said Ump. "You're showing them that a black man can be as responsible as anyone else. Lots of people don't realize that."

"Then they'll find out," said Ralph quietly.

Ralph Bunche was certainly not famous when the war ended in 1945, but he was known among people in the government. They knew that he was brilliant. They knew that he prepared himself and found out about things and understood what was going on. In short, they knew that he was responsible, and that he could make other people be responsible, too.

Because he was known for these qualities, Ralph was asked to help draw up the charter for the United Nations.

"This is terrific!" cried Ralph. "It's my dream coming true! At last we'll have a place where people from all nations can meet to talk over their problems!"

"It's about time!" declared Ump.

For a time it looked as if the United Nations might not work out. In 1947, when the international organization was still new, a war started in Palestine because of disagreements over the new nation of Israel.

Trygve Lie was Secretary-General of the United Nations and he called Ralph. "You are diplomatic," he told Ralph. "You talk gently, but when you talk, people listen. You can make people behave responsibly. Can you try to get the Arabs and the Jews to stop fighting and sign a peace treaty?"

"This is going to be a tough one," said Ump. "The Arabs and the Jews don't like each other very much. You'll have a very hard time getting them to agree."

"I have to try," said Ralph, as he packed his suitcases. "If the U.N. fails to make peace this time, it may never again be able to function as a peace-making agency."

The meetings between the Arabs and the Jews were held in neutral territory, on the island of Rhodes in Greece. Ralph worked long hours there. He pleaded with both sides to make peace. Sometimes he was angry. Often he was tired. He missed Ruth, and he wanted to be at home. But he wouldn't give up.

"You're some umpire!" said Ump.

"I hope so," declared Ralph. Then he called the delegates together for one final meeting. It was a meeting that lasted all day and all night. Everyone was exhausted, but Ralph wouldn't let anyone leave. He kept the men talking. And because they knew him and trusted him—because he was responsible—he was able to make them responsible, too.

At last, as the sun rose over Rhodes, the treaty was signed! Ralph Bunche had ended the war in Palestine, and the United Nations had been able to keep the peace.

When Ralph went home from Rhodes, crowds of people met him at the airport. There was a tickertape parade through Manhattan, and a visit with President Truman at the White House. There was even a trip to Los Angeles, where people turned out by the thousands for "Ralph Bunche Day."

Then Ralph was told that he would be given one of the greatest honors in the world—the Nobel Peace Prize!

"Wouldn't Grandma be proud of you!" said Ump.

Ralph knew she would have been, and the thought made him happy. He was even happier to know that he had been responsible. He had helped bring peace to Palestine, and so he had helped save the United Nations. He had seen what needed to be done, and he had taken care of it.

When you see something that needs to be done, do you take care of it? If you do, you're responsible, and people are responsible to you, too. And chances are that this might make you happier.

Just like our good friend Ralph Bunche.

The End

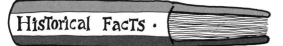

One of the world's leading scholars in the field of race relations, Ralph Johnson Bunche was a key figure in the establishment of the United Nations. In 1950 he was awarded the Nobel Peace Prize for mediating a settlement of the Palestinian War between the new state of Israel and the Arab nations.

Ralph Bunche was born in Detroit, Michigan, on August 7, 1904. He was the son of Fred Bunche, a barber, and Olive Agnes Johnson Bunche, whose father had been born a slave.

The Bunche family moved to Albuquerque, New Mexico, in 1915 because Ralph's mother had developed rheumatic fever and his father had contracted tuberculoses. The Bunches hoped to benefit from the warm, dry climate of the Southwest. While he lived in Albuquerque, Ralph met Miss Emma Sweet, a teacher who inspired him to become a superior student.

Ralph's grandmother, Lucy Johnson, was also tremendously influential in shaping his life. He described her as, "the strongest woman I ever knew, even though she stood less than five feet high." Lucy Johnson took charge of Ralph and his sister after their parents died, and she was the one who urged Ralph to complete his education. He had doubts about continuing in school after he graduated from Jefferson High in Los Angeles in 1922, but his grandmother encouraged him to accept a scholarship to the University of California at Los Angeles.

At U.C.L.A., Ralph displayed the tremendous discipline and great energy which were to characterize his entire career. He was a star on three championship varsity basketball teams, and he played football and baseball. He took part in various debating contests, and when he graduated in 1927 he was a member of Phi Beta Kappa and took his degree *summa cum laude*.

From U.C.L.A., Ralph went to Harvard University for a master's degree in government. He then became an instructor in political science at Howard University in Washington, D.C. At Howard he met and married Ruth Harris. After teaching at Howard for four years, he returned to Harvard to begin work on his doctorate. In 1934 he became the first Negro to receive a Ph.D. in political science.

Ralph continued teaching at Howard, and also continued studies of the social conditions of

RALPH BUNCHE
1904–1971

people in the United States, England and Africa. He soon became known to people in government as someone who knew all there was to know about colonial peoples. He worked for the Office of Strategic Services during World War II, and later for the State Department, and in 1946 he became director of the United Nations trusteeship division.

In 1948 Ralph Bunche replaced Count Folke Bernadotte who had been chief mediator of the UN Palestine Commission. Bernadotte had been assassinated while trying to negotiate a treaty between the Israelis and the Arab leaders. After Ralph took his place, the negotiations were moved from Palestine to neutral territory on the island of Rhodes. There Ralph used all of his diplomatic skills to convince the two factions to make peace. He worked around the clock many times talking to the leaders of the two groups and dictating memos on the progress of the talks. The peace which he negotiated was to last for twenty years.

During his lifetime, Ralph Bunche had the respect and praise of the world. No doubt this was important to him. But what must have been even more important was the knowledge that he had done what he had set out to do. If he had failed at Rhodes—if he had given in to weariness or anger, the war in Palestine could have continued. More lives would have been lost. And the United Nations might have been crippled forever as a peacekeeping force.

The ValueTale Series